The Owl Inside

The Owl Inside

Ivy Ireland

PUNCHER & WATTMANN

First published in 2020
Published by Puncher and Wattmann
PO Box 279
Waratah NSW 2298

http://www.puncherandwattmann.com
puncherandwattmann@bigpond.com

NATIONAL
LIBRARY
OF AUSTRALIA

A catalogue entry for this book is available from the National Library of Australia.

ISBN   9781925780727

Cover design by Miranda Douglas
Typesetting by Morgan Arnett
Printed by Lightning Source International

Contents

III

for Poppy May

I

'I was a strong soul. Look, I will change everything, all the meanings! I thought.'

— Anne Carson

The Owl Inside

It was the owl who called me outside.
Boobook, if I know my owls. And I know my owls.
Nothing too mystical about it;
this was a reminder to take out the bins.
Green bin. And regular. I near sprained my ankle
dragging the too-heavy grass clippings up the too-steep drive.
In the dark. I terrified the possum with my clatter. We jumped.
His landing more graceful than mine. He wasn't hauling a bin.
In fact, it was numinous: scorpion moon in a cloud ring,
bleeding out into the mottled sky like thoughts through an
empty evening. If no one else felt the connection: owl, bin, ring,
then the revelation is solely mine. And that is as it should be.
Afterwards, I stood statue still
in the small woods behind the solemn house;
my chest too bare in this near-cold,
absorbing moonlight like a witch.
I sought to record the sound of the owl
to play back to you later –
once I had caught it, I realised I never would.

Crossing the Sun

All that is true at once:
sea ice melting close by while
we fall in love. How leaves,
also falling, now reveal
Myna birds, exiting branches
as though they, too, are
discarded fronds. Diving down,
returning – towards what –
as though anything could
remain of what was. Illusion
pervades this place, leaving
nothing – everything –
but this endless *trace* inside,
the yearning to make it material.
The apparition sounds:
major fifths chasing
minor sevenths;
intoning endlessly,
looped through
struggling synapses.
The mind cannot know
where to put this, only
the sacrosanct body knows;
and not fully then.

Spotted Pardalote

The notion falls
back down to Earth:
unexpected coughing fit,
a ghost against your neck.

Just sitting there,
looking in to look out,
minding nothing but
your own small business,
you get hit with
the thought's return.

A flicker of some
tiny chirpers
flit and flare past
this aspect, in particular.
Headache birds
in breeding season:
their pitch is a gong.
Return to now.

Then the slow,
meticulous rise of
spirals of gnats.
Dew-lined spider web
dazzling in new light,
two days since Solstice.

You've come here to barely notice,
to explore the soft buzz of quarks.

A trickle of cyclists
dismount by your bench.

Grins trickle down to dirt,
praising sweat, miles,
their own endorphins.

Stillness breaks,
chirpers scuttle,
gnats scatter,
the notion
forces its way in again —
 you might as well name it.

Betrayal: that secrets
cause cell-death,
carve themselves into the liver
once the etched-over heart
has been etched out.

Clouds like discarded
wads of chewing gum
splatter through the now
pavement-grey sky.

This panorama is so close
to what you needed;
all this here is so *almost there*,
you might have arrived at
the pith of it.

You give in,
sigh,
leave the lookout
to those on a high,
begin the slow descent,
a question folded inside:

how can the absence
of one other –
among seven billion others –
influence any outcome
in any significant way?

Grey Is Not Your Colour

In this light, the sky is folded hand towels
in the inexpensive hotel lobby:
neutral grey. Speckled egg shell.
Like this all day, as though
the cloud-towels are close: they will
fall off the God-shelf, right onto, in particular,
your head. Whose fault will that be?
After all, you are ruining this day by driving too fast.
And too far. Just to escape the oppression.
Of thoughts, sure, and of more than that:
of the held-back heart. It is unfair to say
you can't be told what to do. You had planned to
exit the vehicle, wander the wild places,
leave something important behind there. Yet
every turn-off seems to circle you around
back to beckoning highways, endless broken
white lines. Most times, you can follow instructions
to a tee, but with every infinitesimal beat of this
inferior replacement heart — the one you
popped in like you were prompted to
when your own tender core got too
unruly — something glorious and expansive
dies. This is criminal, worse than your driving.
And so. Instead of burying it out there under ironwood,
you must grab your own wild heart in your wicked fist
and shove it back in. This will not be easy,
considering the weather and the fact that you
gouged it out with the shaft of a wedge-tailed eagle feather.
Yet you must make your beat-machine work again. Not for
petty notions of quashed love, but for others who will see
grit glowing through the grey towel clouds. And follow along.

Sea Eagles

Out there beyond all this endless egging on
spins a diamond-core planet with beings

being the days away, just like us —
but much better at it, naturally.

Neither you nor I will ever comprehend
anything about their daily rotations.

Let this be some comfort,
immensity.

But let's stop unpacking the macrocosm,
or this wall we build to quell the calamitous

will collapse into nothing
and —

If you would like to complete that line,
do so — perhaps it will bear its own weight

and leave its own imprint
no matter how many times I press delete.

Let's eject psychobabble, find a lake to walk beside.
In stride, beneath lorikeets swearing at me

in particular. Before you ask I know why —
because I am writing in first person again

all these years after I renounced it
and scribbled over all that was visceral.

The lorikeets do not appreciate these adjectives;
the lorikeets beg me to leave this alone.

So I do. But then I'm left with thoughts of
aliens and money being poured into Space X,

which almost makes me glad inside –
as though I could believe in salvation via sky.

Meanwhile the child and the other chores
rush in to make sure I can ignore

the agitation within in favour of
the daily soap bubbles without.

Yet who would want dreamed-up
diamond core beings

when there could be warmth in the morning
between soft cotton sheets;

when there could be Jack Gilbert
instead of Cats of Instagram.

And if love can't come into this
first person can also politely take its leave.

Now. See her here, alone amongst lorikeets
eerily silent and staring

right into her lake within,
yes, right through it

as though they had the eyes of sea eagles
who have seen it all many times over

and are still sad for one human woman,
to be so transparent in iniquity

that almost any bird could see
the many microplastics

drifting through her waters,
choking desires at will.

How We Will Live

This morning's task is to cleave truth from twaddle
here in the guts of the invisible plenitude.

Dissect the glare of this early morning stormfront,
balance these pitiless winds against impending calm.

Now make it all connect – to what – in a
singular rage of electricity.

In the aftermath, things remain tired and old
especially when lit by rainbow revelation.

This is just your mood. After all, it's not every day
you are woken up early by a storm plus a dawn digger.

Someone is out there in the squall gloaming, burying the
husk of the horse who lives at the end of your street. Lived.

It is every day you are woken up early
out here in the coal mining suburbs.

Yet this interment balanced beneath storm divided by dawn
creates an equation far too complex for the sleepy mind to crack.

Sometimes you think the dead's biggest miracle is not
falling through their gossamer Otherworld back into Earth.

You wouldn't be surprised to wake up tomorrow to find
the old horse returned, glaring at you with that primal eye he has. Had.

Discovering empty hells in the vast multiverse must be
as harrowing as recognising the one waiting for us here.

Considering the rough-chance required for abiogenesis
anywhere else will make your synapses spin.

And while we are on the subject of that sort of thing,
what do you know about the other land, the dead?

By now you've seen your share of caskets –
sorrow thrives in regularity – yet what is gone?

Stopped organs leave pause, but you can't for the life of you
recall ever being lightless, crossed out, not there.

Surely the old horse et al just slip on through into a parallel space-time;
another now. Hopefully less suffocating than this one.

This learned article claims we won't find life on Mars while
we are too busy bickering over what constitutes life here on Earth.

You loved that old horse – Teddy – yet all day long will forget
his new lack of that determined spark that once jumped his heart.

You will search for him out the kitchen window.
You might traipse to the lounge-room for a better view.

You will witness drag-marks mapping his final choreography,
you will watch the dank, dark mud keel and roil in this rain.

Recall. Recoil. Death takes a while, long past it's seeming,
to condense any sort of reality bubble around the gone thing.

Mars One prepares for something like death. No rockets yet, but
astronauts lined up for the one-way ticket to more unknowable.

Don't pretend you didn't audition. Don't compare this
ill-conceived rush forward with your own dirge toward death.

Today's task is to beg whatever waits past the present
that the invisible plenitude won't eat it all up right now:

dead horse, vital Martians, those arrows of prayer you
shoot at both ends of the unintelligible equation.

Small Town Big Wet

that's how it goes with boons from the sky
                         it's not raining then it is
who can fathom that mystical moment of initial impact
                         the musk of wet stone slides into the absolute
what does it matter if we comprehend any of these
                         miniscule milliseconds of pure shift
it will never signify if we comprehend the absolute
                         inside this simple fact of rain
this one who is five says it comes from the mountains and the sea
                         the mountains and the sea mummy simple
in her lexicon the glorious axiom simple ends argument
                         nothing more to say please don't try to say it
simple also means that she won definitively
                         she is not yet quite sure just what
this is the cosmogony of late spring drought relief
                         when we dance in it we are only bodies
and sometimes the day wins this way
                         simple
passes through all ephemera
                         no need to make a sign over itself
leaves the bones of what has taken place
                         we can pick through those later
yet this boon now slicks our bodies
                         small blessing in this perfect only moment

Dream Therapy

1.

never should it be said
she left for the last time
in the slow afternoon
down the puddled street
beyond his picket fence
and froze
in the wake of what
she had always known as
a grey heron
which is in fact a
white-faced heron
with another bird's wing
likely another heron
at least that's how it appeared
snapped in its beak
which is more correctly
a bill

she closed her eyes
checked again
the white-faced heron
flicked its neck
the grotesque appendage
dangled between them
like a migraine aura

neither of the participants
not woman nor bird
moved

perhaps this wing was instead

flayed frog
which would make sense
but as her heart venerates
the nonsensical
now as ever
in her view of events
birds will eat birds

a macabre moment
which is more correctly
augury
why can't she see it

2.

that night she dreams
the darkness in again
where she wakes
but does not wake

tears forming rivulets
and she can't connect dots
until another self
out wandering the night
comes roaming home
screams meanings
in her own ear
in her own words
that are not words
so why call them that

one night terror
is largely unremarkable
every now and again

this night
post cannibalistic heron
grey on grey street
after five times
waking weeping
watch her levitate
from the bed
hover along the hall
tear-creeks forming
cracks down her cheeks

when she returns
mind claims it was self
in those dreams
wearing his face
mouthing nothings
with a wing in mouth
perhaps articulating
the true felony
from a known future
quickly becoming past

some bird eat bird
that this body
in this bed
which is more correctly
the crime scene
can't catch up with
just now
and probably never will

Erupt

a question through these years
tiny bubbles through stone
beneath unsuspecting surface

why don't you erupt
mar something
leave a stain
or volcano
some tiny chemical collision
somewhere close
at the very least
please

why is it all so still now
when we did in fact form the full circle
shaped our sphere with warped assumptions
buried enquiry inside this geode

even kookaburras fall silent
when they want to be
witness this slow soar into branch
so shaded by Jacaranda fronds
they might not even be there

crocodiles can be on you
before you know it
nobody mention whales
upwards out of – where
to surface in this Jesus Christ
bloody hell football
field sized happening

you are outsized like that

silently sliding through all exterior
yet increasingly subtext

hypertext objects
but what is hypertext anyway
I mean you are magma
housed beneath layers of stone
to the microscopic this is massive

I'm pretty sure we don't hear
tectonic plates
gliding over and grating
against each other
pushing and shoving until
collision everything
falling into fissure

so it's no surprise we would
end up in bed
eons after the collapse of
the notion of continuity

is it enough to leave behind
that silent creep-up of tide
as gas bubbles in ancient ice
release Anthrax into the melt

when these silicon and shale
Earth-curtains
are first knocked against
it is a friendly nudge
against a tiny fault

a barely-noticed prick into
bubbles through stones and yet

I shudder to think of
the grand scale loss to come

Trampoline

When this whole world terminates, it does so
spectacularly. And that's when you say
there was never any kick to it, no actual
grandeur. Spring, hitting like summer:
cut lawns, possum poo on the trampoline.
Hose the kid off too while you are at it. Make a melon
daquiri, bring the soccer ball inside before the
sun forces it to fade away into nothing. The
highs – grab the branch – the lows – watch the
sewerage cap – and the fine static electricity
in her winged hair. *Zap. Boing.* The jump-squelch sounds like
subordination; it all falls apart before the chance to mark
passage, build a safety grid, bear witness against. Is it to be up now or
down? And who shall say which or when? A sad little ghost,
beckoning you out towards the shade beneath the
mango tree, holds the truth of the matter in its eyes.

II

'So what if it all took place
Silently inside you?'
            – Gregory Orr

Hedge Identity Politics

Out the plane window, arrows of hedge, intersecting.
They do it subtly here, as though collision is purely incidental,
as though asking and answering could be one.
As though what remains: that crush where they meet
as though they didn't at all mean to – that immediacy – is all there is.
On the ground, a robin in song. His hops through hedge are liquid metal,
perhaps mercurial, but more akin to smelted copper.
You have returned here – home – to ask one question. No.
You have journeyed back north – away – to discover
the one question worth asking now;
just what remains to be asked, considering.
A tiny blade of sun slices through fog, overexposing
incandescent green, blinding against the gloom-ridden grey.
You didn't see that one coming. Terrifying, the joy a small spark brings.
What to make of this: the answer to prayer? A punch in the face?
Here, inside the closing circle, where all this springtime drive was
always leading, it could well be either. Probably both.
The whole Easter mess more sense in the north.
This is your second seeding season this cycle; the last one held more heat,
less blossom. Still, you circumvent the contagion of renewal,
twice-potent with expectation that something really ought to shift.
This genetic funk you carry through eternity, holy in constancy,
knows beyond knowing just what it is to set out against asking questions,
legitimate or loathsome; to take everything as far away as possible,
towards penalty disguised as exotic promise, through terror,
boon, jungle or salt. And here, now, these binding chains, these
nucleotides of this particular double helix downward spiral dance,
have the gall to return home – away – to this tangle of blackthorn,
gorse, hawthorn and heather that once wrapped itself around your name.
You have returned here, now you are so far past asking, to beg these
hedges, these instances of intersection, to take the space-charged
quarks of this moment's body back into their embrace.
Some forward movement must pause, right here at the root,

to account for all this anesthetised ancestral continuing.
You have come to demand this twisted wedge of witch-trees
snatch all iniquity caused by the avoidance of enquiry
from this family history, and never, ever give it back.

The Lagan

thick black ooze moves
gnats flick
above and above
right to fear
what is rising up
from beneath

this viscous murk
would embower
bury me under
as I sit here
all this long while
claiming
the river's only depth
is my own reflection

unlike other
lovers of shadows
my *mallacht*
is this peering through
what stares back
also wondering

another curse I claim
is covetousness
I want this miasma
beneath beyond
between
gnats above and
slush gods
deep below
to call my own

some subtle spirit
must shape the Lagan
some *sídhe*
that might be kin
to this one self
who peers back
against all this
being known

Spring in the Wicklow Mountains

ten thousand meadow pipits
beating wings against
this rhythm of
crackling gorse
carelessly lit

unnamed fish
leap from the deep dark
belly of the valley
at the very notion

you can believe it
and later
when you replay this scene
over and over
your will to
separate yourself out
from thornbush
from faery tree
from heather
chestnut oak and
ash
turns to stone

asleep
in this druid's oak
clear within
you are not now
what you were
just yesterday

Forest Lacuna

at first he is the quality of light
on rainforest floor
        dappled shifting uncertain

she is one small seedling
reaching one slim limb
        towards gleaming

. . .

past noon he is
that darkening
        fringe of leaf-litter

she is the twitter of
tiny wings beating through
        thickets of twigs

. . .

by night he is
smooth black creek stones
        worn to gloaming beneath moon

she is water eroding
a rock-thick need to name mystery
        eternal things whispering

. . .

come dawn they are gone

News Rhythm

And when I consider the war —
this war that war which war all wars —
I see a maudlin Falstaff
humming out the headlines.

"An Axis of Evil"
is sung to the tune of
"I'm Walking on Sunshine."

The eye in my mind brings him back,
the café where I worked —
off the books —
the both of us there, every single day.
Me unwrapping the Belfast Telegraph,
him translating, transposing, warbling
out of tune with such precise timing.

All of the songs we'd heard too many times before.
All of the headlines fit the rhythm far too perfectly.

I see his hips swinging as he sings,
fingers tracing the propaganda machine,
rough living eyes twinkling wildly —
those sparks against my eager glance.

I named him Solid Gold Hits Guru,
coating the indigestible
with easy glossy nonsense —
or was it the other way around?

Now when I can't avert
the eye in my mind
fast enough to survive

and accidently read a headline,
years and countries later – same war –
I provide my own plastic pop:
sugary ditty to accompany atrocity.

Take It

If you were granted those harmonies of heaven:
the next Ezekiel, used up by a god,
but oh so relevant while
flayed alive by angel breath –
what could possibly follow after?

Back on earth you might
make melody
on the odd occasion
out of that otherwise
silent, judgmental throat.
You may even dream dreams,
practice legitimate magic:
a truly prophetic
figure of the space age.

Yet sleep studies have proved,
definitively,
dreams dive into us via the
Warm Hot Intergalactic Medium.
This rescinded mind junk
– the progeny of WHIM –
should also have the decency to
fuck back off to the great nothing
when it is politely asked to leave.

If science finds the mind
and all the benefactors
throw parties for it –
girls in cakes or fairies in bread –
villains will still attend.
One powerful conservative
will get offended,

the mind might get kicked out
or kidnapped for ransom
and could well wind up
back where it all began.

Another war-in-heaven,
a single cell
upended under a slide
beneath a microscope
transferred to a petri dish;
some superhero above
throwing lightning,
spouting utter nonsense
since the now multiplying cell
is perfectly too tired to   .
produce nonsense for itself.
Inappropriate nucleotides
will form the thin red line
over and over.

Again and again,
the way out appears
as a dim outline
just on the edge of eyes;
a faint harmony of heaven,
as far away as those
mountains of mysticism.
Like everything worth venerating,
it will need to be translated
and then transfigured.
Don't just sit there, take it, take it in,
take it back, take it through.
When granted those harmonies of heaven,
save nothing for later. Take it all.

Household Accounting

Four boys on four bikes,
fourth street of your walk,
forth hour of the afternoon,
fourth day of the week.

Uncanny:
four pelicans claim the sky.

'I'm that one!'
Boy out in front claims
the premier bird.
'No, *I'm* that one!'
The very same bird,
runner-up child.
'You always get the best one, I'm… '
Third boy.

More bickering,
dwarfing a small voice:
'I'm that one over there.'

There's always one.

You glance up.
The furthest away flyer,
almost invisible now, off-kilter,
defies the built-in compass,
chasing solely the arcane way.

Fourth boy, otherwise unremarkable,
follows potency,
worships unheralded augury,
in the same way you do –

both of you will sing the wordless hymn later
when asked to defend your singular stance.

Easy to name it glorious,
deliberate mystification,
but for the cumulative cost of
choosing the peculiar path home –
the unaccounted-for way –
time and time again.

The price is well known to you,
data inked into your well-lined skin.
No point warning fourth boy,
such as he will not take heed. Not yet.

Instead, return home
along well-manicured footpaths,
forgive all your precious things
for being just so and nothing else –
for lining themselves up to
create symmetrical shapes.
Clutch them close,
hold to the ordering principle of
personal daily habit.

Forgive yourself for choosing the
straight way to small victory;
for finding safety in the folds of
clean towels crisping up the linen press.

All you can do with a home is
hold space for overlapping worlds –
the mediocre and the mundane
spoon neatly up against
the cosmic and the absurd.

All you can do with containment is
document, name, account for:
write out what's yours,
minus the bifurcations of chaos,
solve what small equations you can,
then own the blessing in tiny repetitions.

Next time you walk,
don't account for any of it.
Leave the boys on bikes
to race through the safe streets,
flee to the patch of wood
not yet eaten up by kit-homes.
Move beyond late afternoon
sun-blazed pelicans,
inch toward dim eldritch owl-light:
darker, less certain,
yet still within the reach of
those well-lit windows of home.

Baptistry Ceiling Mosaic

here's Christ with Poseidon
a coin slot Mary
she lights up
she lights up
for a fee

overly ornate
here's some old sculptor-saint
tile after tile
face speckled
gold dust and cobalt blue
mixing gods with ceramics

the old ones first
Jesus next
then Mary
phased in on a whim
yet remaining since
forever began

but this mosaic maker
hanging from this roof
all life long
neck shot to pieces
moulding myths from fragments

this mansion for the gods
once a den of pantheistic vice
now the baptismal river of Christ

overlaid truths
prophet after prophet
plastering epiphanies

sheltered by simplicity

something right here
something concerned with
cultish chronologies
should be articulated
set in stone
left to mould the next minions

yet who is willing
I am all agape
unwilling to forge
my own mistakes

to add to the collective guilt
this Bacchanalian Bathhouse is
slowly sinking to shale
four floors
since the last millennia

holy Father Time
is getting rid of it

meanwhile this Christ
twinned to that old god
is rising through the extensions

this house of worship
is on the rack
out of all proportion
the good gods upwards
pushing the Empyrean
the bad gods downwards
to where we all must go

and someplace else
between Hades and the angels
sits youth and wonder
adjudicating all

obvious
unappreciative
more ignorant than the
Ostrogothic sculptor

unwilling to prophesy
or state a firm position
searching in my pockets
for that last gold coin

Knock

with various saints and
a starry lamb in tow
the Blessed Virgin
must have questioned
her holy wisdom
calling on a farm
unannounced
in the dead of night
down through the rain
county Mayo 1879

everybody else
was exiting the blight
yet in she came
through the veils
far above this wild blasted earth
a pure gossamer glory

the exact representation
the whiter than white shrine
makes eyes water in the rare full sun
shafting through those high windows
meant to touch all that is holy
and they do

a remote area
is any part of Sligo not remote
smells of deep bog
sounds like the disembodied
voice of Yeats in the British library
resounding fiercely through time
appears like black earth splotched with
famine graves and Ogham stones

it wasn't nothing
Mary turning up like she did
impoverished grannies
died from the shock of it
the Marian Apparition
carved out a future whirlwind
infrastructure nightmare
millions of pilgrims every year

across the road from the shrine
a small shop offers tea and trinkets
appearing out of the stark July sun like
the sitting room of an eccentric old aunt
nobody remembers to visit

and who am I to say one word about it
chasing Yeats's Tarot tower
lake of wherever a short drive away
even if I was Yeats in a past life
that doesn't make me Mother Mary now
nor the Queen of the *sídhe*
we all necessarily bow before
at the unmarked earth mound next door

and so I throw my
Mary-shaped plastic bottle
purchased in the tea shop
under the holy water bubbler
just like all the rest
just in case
I fill it to the brim

this is more than reverence
this is genetic memory
the sheer craving

for there to be something
for something to be more
than my own story's small miracle
and it is

I cart that plastic Mary
full of holy water
home across the seas
don't declare it at customs
her crown is the lid
in a sense I would scalp her
every time I seek blessing

she sits unopened on my desk
which is a shrine
ten years or more in stasis
the water slowly evaporates
yet the trace remains
for some emergency
just as potent like this
perhaps homeopathic
hope and pray

the wonder of it also sits
somewhere inside my gut
a second appendix of holy mystery
entirely ready to burst open inside
the potential of that
spontaneous rapture combustion
of sudden visitation
is life threatening really
though we wouldn't be without it

Acorn

Working this through, then,
in the freezer sits an oak seed.
Grant this disk of vital spark
true wintering, allow time
to do what time will:
take in a tiny death, magic it to
august life. Give it over to the quickening.
Pluck it out for planting in spring.
When the tree sprouts, this suspension,
this freezing over, this
nothing all the time empty
stillness –
what is nothing –
will have been one universal
instant, one essential
delay. Necessity. Nothing more.
Nothing less.
Don't smirk at this,
as though you do not need to be told.
As though that rule is now redundant,
as though your grief is more.
As though it were all so simple,
naming loss. Giving word to this
deep howl in the rotting moss forest.
As though it were human to
allow, after pause, life.
As though one could simply
mark the darks of solstice,
dutifully map the returning line of light
along the passage tomb floor, take
heed as ancestors all the while whisper,
'thus and so, thus and so,'
and navigate towards remedy.

As though you will ever
leave off your keening
for the sake of scientific fact.
Still. A life pod graces
the suburban kitchen freezer:
enforced cryonic suspension.
May cold hell hold enough deep magic
to fire the new shoot through.

Spring Green

Casually drops. Pulls shapes.
Discovers her own fresh scent,
one that doesn't play well with others.
Spring green owns the game.
As for me, I slept through the night –
there is deep mercy in forgetting.
Morning, and boxes full of grown humans
work away beyond my window. I play truant;
all this blossoming requires a witness.
Another self, projected backwards through
burning futures, remembers what it means to be
in this moment, with a borrowed bathrobe
and a tiny golden secret. The good kind.

III

'When the men leave me, they leave me in a beautiful place.'
— Linda Gregg

Heat

Merely the season for heat. And by this is meant anything but acceptance.
Passing time cursing contingency, sugar-coating surrender.
Only a complete giving over will suffice here.
And that is never going to happen.
Autumn signals more summer. A piano croaks in the background,
one with not enough skill for it attempts Liszt.
And suddenly this is me: a teen shoved against the piano.
Emotional eagerness above and against technicality.
The willing distortion of sensibility over sense.
This memory hurts. Ire gurgles through my gut at the image:
butchering Beethoven back then,
exploding the trill, stretching beyond impossible chord progressions.
Bold dynamic and torrid touch, never enough temperance.
Sitting in that back room in the cold house in silence.
Stoic. Determinedly not playing scales,
though it might have warmed fingers, granted some comfort.
There is a great discipline within moodiness,
a core exhaustion in never giving anyone what they want.
Refusing the closure of the perfect cadence, scoffing at the tentative
openings of the imperfect. Banging out bone-jarring fifths to sixths
for the sake of why not. Smashing Pumpkins in the contraband Walkman.
Why should this shard be plucked from the past?
Here in this blistering backyard of dirt and dead grass,
feet sting on stones beside three loads of washing.
Inside, disparate groceries wait to become school lunch,
the child throws a pot of glitter into the carpet and
the bell will sound before anything sorts itself out.
And this me out here: this set of baby-blighted breasts,
deep-set eyes from the terrifying sleeplessness of care,
now abandoned in all this breathless mediocrity
for the mythic glory of the twenty-years-younger replacement,
fresh from school herself. Probably butchering her own Beethoven
in the back room of the family home,

waiting for the saviour to speed out of mundanity to collect her.
He will plonk her down behind his smile on the brand-new Moto Guzzi.
Another replacement item. This steed, too, is mythic in proportion.
He will wave to her father as they burn
out into the new day as though he is not himself a father,
overtaking the milestone of midlife as he weaves through traffic.
As though, by afternoon, Indian summer, we could all revert,
go back to bathe in the fresh dawn dew of Spring.
Disjunction to section endings and on through the repetitions
so fast, and with such a deep degree of difficulty,
his seduction syzygies rivalled a Liszt Étude.
I might have to take up the piano again just to win at something.
Meanwhile, Great Mother, goddesses of all deep myth:
where does one go to expel this heat? The bottom of the
dirty clothes basket? The cool cement floor of the laundry?
Where is the space for the stark, hot-sick fit of pique
that breaths down the neck of initial despair?
Hot-sick: term coined by my daughter in the car, grasping
compound words, in an attempt to describe dizziness —
the perfect pearl in all this ungraciousness.
Hot-sick: vertiginous, vomitus, too many layers on,
accelerating into all the godforsaken bends, as though
we are the ones on the back of the bike.
Hot-sick: this teeth-clenching, jaw-dropping fury,
fusing through, wave after wave.
Then negation. Pause. Realising I do not, even today,
hold the emotional discipline to master Liszt.
This heat! The sheets dry as they hit the line.
Worse still is the plinking piano, my memory layered onto it,
and the unceasing voice accompanying it all;
unfolding from the manifold movements of women's history
to find itself solely my own. This small song claims
hot-sick is nothing but non-acceptance: denial of that
bullet-dodging forsakenness of single-motherhood.
So much out there in the heat is worse than this.

I head back inside to vacuum up the glitter.

Single Mum

The objects scattered across her room are galaxies
rising up, hovering for an instant where they are, then
flinging themselves out the door, flying
by my fixed presence in the hallway –
always too fast, with far too much velocity. I can't catch them;
I never could. They have done this to me all along.
Teething toys to Barbie dolls, Goodnight Moon to Matilda,
Beetle to Scrabble. There were nappies, once.
Who can forget breasts squirting milk across the cosmos?
Spew rags and crapped jumpsuits. Sleeplessness – yes,
when a good night's rest took off, that was a one-way journey, too.
Suggestions, snide comments. Everyone else knowing better, doing more.
Febrile convulsions in Emergency, night-wetting – my bed, my leg – and
preschool paintings on rented walls. The body holds it all, the mind
    cannot.
Now, out beyond the constant giving-over of homework,
dubious BFFs, extra-curricular whatever afternoons driving
absolutely wherever into Friday night school-mum wines,
these constellations of a life still push past my wide-open eyes,
speed by my O-gape mouth of quiet surprise. Who will close my lips?
Who will put these things back in their place before this tiny world
    comes home?
All this clinging to edges, clutching at an expansion that cannot be
    comprehended,
let alone ended. I'd cease, but the objects don't. Stop?
The future crone me, still hovering in the hallway,
expecting to get hit with all this endless shooting stuff,
cackles at the very notion of severance.

How to Protect the Lungs

Inhalation of ash is the new normal
as I fashion myself Jungian,
transpersonal, still able to scribble and scrawl
what dreams are left to me,
while my hands wrinkle and curl to crone,
and the forest burns. All forest,
not just this one here by the garden.
I'd watch and wait, evacuate,
but it's far too late for that now.
Instead, I code the Pantone:
666-Apocalypse, this iron red sky at noon.
The great age of the Millennial,
no longer dirty thirties cruising the Apps –
we've merged into Millenarian.
Self-flagellants in the suburbs in the smoke,
backs beaten raw with single-use plastic guilt, upcycling fails;
the cold congeal of a non-free-range drive-thru breakfast.
Down at the oval there's a ghost-dance or cargo-cult –
ascension by meditation in tool sheds disguised as spaceships,
or could it be the other way around.
I gather with the rest of them on rooftops at dawn,
waiting for whatever comes next,
howling out the absurdity of all school bells now
the soup-sky of dust and bone-bits and burnt leaves
has clogged up lungs until the voice is a raw cough –
and then silence. It has come to this.
There's a netherworld waiting, just beyond
these prophetic dreams I've almost stopped mapping out.
A collective unconscious of underground angels
granting passage through fire-fuelled cognitive dissonance,
offering ascension through ash and mire and on out the door
as though future fields could feel green,
as though the heavens could ever again know Yves Klein blue.

But like stars above air pollution, future fantasy feels extinct.
In deepest sorrow, I fashion myself practical, line up to buy
a box of breathing masks from Bunnings. The serious kind.

I Am Not Doing Anything

And when my heart for all this ending
shrinks to the size of a frozen pea,
and when I want to close the blinds,
Netflix and chill until I forget there is any ocean,
let alone this one, charging forth to eat us all,
 — too trite to say it serves us right —
I make myself recall the birds, fallen,
the bandicoots and desert rats, the frogs I
wish I had kissed into princes before they left
what now remains of Earth.
Bats. Koalas. Rivers of fish. I make my mind bring up
beaches: shore erosion felling homes, forests: now ash and dust,
sky: daily smoke haze. I could list extinctions and endangerments
until our eyes burst with the build-up of unshed tears,
but this way lies madness, medication
and more endless TV of forgetting.
Episode after episode. When I can no longer turn
the Anthropocene into a HD essay,
recite a readily consumed lists of deaths,
I spend my time reading up on the burden of overwhelm —
this is as useless as everything else.

FOMA Remedy

The greatest accomplishment of this day is
brewing coffee, then sipping herbal tea instead.
There's joy in disavowal, in sitting still, silent at home
while the party of the year rages eagerly nearby –
my name is on the door. I could be the guest of honour.
No matter, here is the bird, again, attacking my baby pine.
Honeyeater: Fierce Persistence is her stage name.
Shooing and scolding again, later, I realise
the boon she seeks is the pale green wool I used
to stake the wayward spine straight, to put things to rights.
She sought to snatch the binding tool, not betray the essence.
I find scissors – not easy in a dreamer's stationary draw –
cut the ties, throw the wool to the grass that wants mowing,
hope Fierce Persistence will spy the gift in the scrubby mire.
The tree shall grow which way it will, the bird shall build her nest.
If this is predictable, why fight so hard to win against anything?
There is an exhale always asserting itself out there, while
I beg, again and again, for special treatment, to not be subject to law,
to ignore all birthdays on a whim.
There is no escaping the remembering that comes right before sleep.
I sip my tea, this one strong with mint. Take joy in this,
pour the cold coffee over vanilla ice-cream for afters.

A Day of Snakes and Brambles

A day of snakes hiding themselves inside brambles,
and I, beside only myself, cannot seem to sort
one from the other. Here, in the thick of it, plucking away endlessly
at the scrub of the subconscious, they appear the same.
Snakes entangle deeply when they mate. Rope knots carving
paths anyone might be taken in by, never to return.
When the snakes separate, how can they know
the skin they now carry is theirs alone?
And brambles: no fruit so sweet as to warrant the wounds.
The cuts and snags of plucking from that wound-up mess.
No need to keep telling the tale of the last bitter harvest.
Next season, I shall leave the fruit to rot and moulder on the vine.
I will keep watch as silent rage – outrage – smoulders on forever,
the burning heart of a nuclear reactor. When this core is exposed, it
    destroys.
No need to belabour the point, but it's not really
burning, is it? More like un-creating:
making worse than nothing of what once was more than all.
I want burning. True entanglement where, when we rise from the ashes,
one is still one, two is just something else standing beside. Clearly the other.
But first to release the reverie haunting this day: tangled brambles,
entwined snakes, slithering out over this smouldering nuclear wasteland.
The remains of what was impacting enough to split the framework of
everything held dear. To smithereens. No need to dissect the allusion.
No one can be expected to fall in love with this dream in their head;
as pointed and blunt as pencils before and after a day of kindergarten.
This thing we do here: when will it end its fission? Not in my lifetime.
I will name this exclusion zone unliveable. Give it over to the snakes
    and brambles.
Meanwhile, what will I do with all this airborne despair?
The half-life of outrage. And where can I possibly move
to escape those neutrinos winding through everything, even now,
so long post-fact. There is no post-fact.

Dead Man

I am full of longing for impossible futures. Any future is thus, now,
considering. In this one, I live in a log cabin, neat,
near the Rockies. My hair is glossy, black and straight. Strong nose.
Alberta, perhaps, perhaps a horse ranch, though we wouldn't call it that
because the horses run free and only come near when they need to.
We never ride those Mustangs, unless they like it, perhaps
once a year in deep snow; blinding white light
flecking up to coat us, too, in a type of blank belonging.
Or perhaps in spring, bareback, mane for reins and wildflowers
crunching under hoof. Always snow somewhere in the distance.
These alps glow so bright white in sunlight;
they remember the names of all of ours who went before
because we were all born beneath them
and did not leave to take anyone else's belonging place –
that would never have occurred to us.
Nobody in that future has ever heard of water restrictions or
forest fires or dead fish in over-heated river systems
or the worst drought recorded or mining magnates or fools
climbing Uluru because nobody ever taught them simple respect.
Yes, I wanted to say stupid fucking white men, Jim Jarmusch.
In this impossible future I even made marriage work;
this is as far from me as being Indigenous Canadian,
though I have dreamed of this, too, many times –
another mixed-race Caucasian exile from the Southern Colonies,
still ignorant and lost, still romanticising snow.

Watching Monks

And I could write a book about
not wanting to write a book about
the way a book comes at you while you sleep
and you have to get it out of you. Vast exorcism required.
There is no Hot Priest from Fleabag here. No Shaman to sing your
  bones back in.
Precisely nothing nearby when you sleep, just the way you like it,
but that cursed book, oozing into everything like some
totalitarian despot you would also be if you could somehow manage
  people.
Don't ask the book to explain itself; it has achieved diagnosis of ADHD,
will use five hundred pages of words when just one would suffice:
  contingency.
No, two words: axiomatic death.
Yet, three words. See? The words keep at it and are legion. The book
  wins.
When monks make a sand mandala,
so precise that deprivation is vindicated, the beauty of it hurts
somewhere deep where your cells are mostly still star.
And yet the killing of the thing, the wiping clean, the bodily purging
  required
to let go of thinking you can achieve anything by sleep or by waking
  up, really
– then letting go of that, too, then doing all of it anyway –
is more than simply beautiful, or even hurtful-glorious.
It is nothing more than everything.
*Get the book out of you all by yourself. Get the book away from yourself
all by yourself,* I chant incessantly. That's the true work.

Dark Moon Gap

there will be
chastened ghost notes
in the gap
just beyond the space
before the next phase

when ringing out
ceases
again and again
echo remains
find that trace
still transpiring
and then
there

gap again

surrender only to this

Don't Follow the Pretty Things

While you were in the hospital, you know, busy with the dying,
shutting things down, staving off the worst of it, shunting last liquids
through your broken shell that doesn't even situate you in space now,
I, across town, was up with the child. Witching hour, wet bed.
Was it nightmare or just general attachment to this plane:
a fight against the paralysis of dreaming.
To open the road, you first have to walk back along it,
probably in reverse, against the ways we are used to here.
Who knows what you saw, then, busy with the dying while I
lived and breathed and pumped my own not yet incorrect chemicals
    around,
sparked those tiny fires through my pulsing grey matter,
guilty from the effort of mining your dying for words,
ashamed of all my endless distractions and reactions,
not knowing how to label a pure feeling.
Would something give me an excuse to stop the mad life here, too,
as I scrubbed and washed and remade the bed, leaving the
peed sheets, blankets, pillow in the bathtub to deal with in the morning.
Singing a lullaby, completely haunted,
though you hadn't formed a ghost, yet. I tried to recall the Tibetan Book,
all that night long, you know, while you were busy with the dying:
how many days to wait, which light to follow, which phantasms to
    ignore,
which ones were the worst dressed up as the best.
The most precious things are all tricks – I read it to the last dead friend.
So I chanted with my mind voice, which can get a better
hold of you where you're headed than the throat one:
don't follow the pretty things, Meg,
take the clear glow road to the next real deal.
Apparently, liberation can't be mistaken for anything else.
No diversions. Don't you ever come back here again.

Tiny Knife

Confessional: I kneel.
It is sudden, this collapse.
There's a pulse of trance. Flickering
out.
A ladder inside,
towards where you reside,
deep in the central image.
The slick of raw egg white,
crushed rose petals,
almond meal.
It is late here.
Some bird cuts through the night.
Tiny knife.
Wings swoop by the
wide open
kitchen sliding door.
Predatory, perhaps,
yet all I sense is
the low growl
ache of the gentle.
I kneel.
Repetition, yes,
yet with new quickening,
an urgency.
It is day somewhere else,
where the parts of you
that are not here, reside.
Don't pull back now.
The questions beg to enter,
refuse passage.
The pulse yearns to get it here,
now. Get it over with.
Allow pause.

No movement against,
only towards. Within.
A tiny night breeze
scratches scalp,
playful.
Phytoncides communicate
ancient things
through dark
between trees —
we can't know about those.
Drive and desire,
who let you in, here,
all these years post fact?
You were so slippery
we didn't feel it coming.
Quite impossible,
this confession.
And yet. I kneel.

Acknowledgements

Poems from this collection have appeared in: *Plumwood Mountain, Silence: The University of Canberra Vice-Chancellor's International Poetry Prize 2019 Anthology, The Blue Nib, Women* of *Words, Messages from the Embers, Verity La's Spirit* of *Home, The Australian Poetry Collaboration, The Canberra Times, The New England Writers Centre Thunderbolt Prize 2018 Anthology.* "The Owl Inside" was runner-up in the University of Canberra's Vice-Chancellor's International Poetry Prize 2019, "Acorn" was short listed for the 2020 Woorilla Poetry Prize, "Crossing the Sun" was longlisted in The University of Canberra's Vice-Chancellor's International Poetry Prize 2019, "Grey is Not Your Colour" won the New England Writer's Centre's Thunderbolt Prize in 2018.

This one's for you, Poppy May – thank you. Thanks also to my parents for all their support and kindness, to Melly and Margie for always being there, and to The Press Bookhouse for all the adventures over the years. Endless gratitude to Brook Emery, without whose close reading and encouragement this book would never have left the shelter of the shadows. Deepest thanks also to Keri Glastonbury and Judy Johnston for the wonderful editorial suggestions, Jenny Blackford for the poetry opportunities and encouragement, David Musgrave for taking a chance on this manuscript, and to the marvellous women of the Workshop Coven and the Newcastle Feminist Poetry Workshop.

www.ingramcontent.com/pod-product-compliance
Lightning Source LLC
Chambersburg PA
CBHW031006090426
42737CB00008B/703